Thank you to the generous team who gave their time and talents to make this book possible:

Authors

Ellenore and Leyla Angelidis

Illustrator

Eyayu Genet

Creative Directors

Caroline Kurtz, Jane Kurtz, and Kenny Rasmussen

Translators

Abdi Mohamed Hassen

Designers

Beth Crow and Kenny Rasmussen

Ready Set Go Books, an Open Hearts Big Dreams Project

ISBN: 979-8844461712
Library of Congress Control Number: 2022914800

Printed in Seattle, WA, U.S.A.

Publication Date: 8/15/22

Head in the Stars

Hami sare

English and Somali

One day, the girl's aunt came home from college.
maalin ayey gabadha
habaryarteed guriga
soo booqatay iyadoo
katimiday dhank kuliyada.

"Come," she said. "I brought a painting to show you why my head is always in the stars."

kaalay waxaan kuu keenay sawire, si aan kuutuso sababta aan mar kasta uga fikiro xidigahee ayey kutidhi gabadhii yarayd.

The girl asked, “Will someone from Ethiopia ever go into space?”

gabadhii yarayd ayaa habaryarteed waydiisay “qof kamid ah dadka Itoobiya matagi doonaa samada?”

"Who knows? Why not you?" her aunt said.

habaryarteed ayaa ugu jawaabtay "yaa garanaya"? adigaba maxaa kuudiidaya?

"When I was your age, I visited Lalibela," her aunt said. "In the night, the moon, stars, and planets were very bright."

gabadha yar habaryarteed ayaa waxay kutidhi “markaan adiga da’daada ahaa waxaan booqday magaalada Laalibeele” dayaxa, xidigaha iyo cirkuba habeenkii waa cadaan.

"I always dreamed of seeing the planets up close," her aunt added.

gabadha yar habaryarteed ayaa tidhi “waxaan markasta ku fikiraa/ riyoodaa inaan arko caalamka inagu wareegsan”.

MERCURY
VENUS
NEPTUNE
MARS
JUPITER
SATURN

Her aunt taught her about seven planets that can be seen from Addis Ababa.

gabadha yar habaryarteed waxay bartay todobo kamid ah meerayaasha inagu xeeran. kuwaas oo ay kamidyihiin meeraha

Mercury, Venus, Mars, Jupiter, Saturn, Uranus, and Neptune.

Merkuri,meeraha Fenas, meeraha Jubiter, Meeraha saterni, meeraha Yuranas iyo Meeraha Nebtuun.

The girl joined her school's Space Club.

gabadhii waxay kamid noqotay ururka dayx gacmeedka dugsigooda.

She and her friends imagined wonders hidden in the sky.

iyada iyo saaxiibadeed waxay sawirteen waxyaabaha layaabka leh eek u dhax qarsoon samada.

Her aunt took her to visit Entoto Observatory and ground station. They were able to see the planets through the telescope there.

habaryarteed ayaa waxay gaysay xarunta baadhista hawada ee Intooto. waxay arkeen meerayaasha inagu xeersan iyagoo adeegsanaya waynayso.

Sometimes they
needed to stay up late.
mararaka qaar
kudaahayeen ilaa
xili danbe.

Sometimes they needed
to wake up early.
mararka qaarna subaxa hore
ayey kici jireen.
Sometimes they needed to get
up in the middle of the night.
mararka qaarna waxay
kici jireen saqda dhaxe
ee habeenkii.

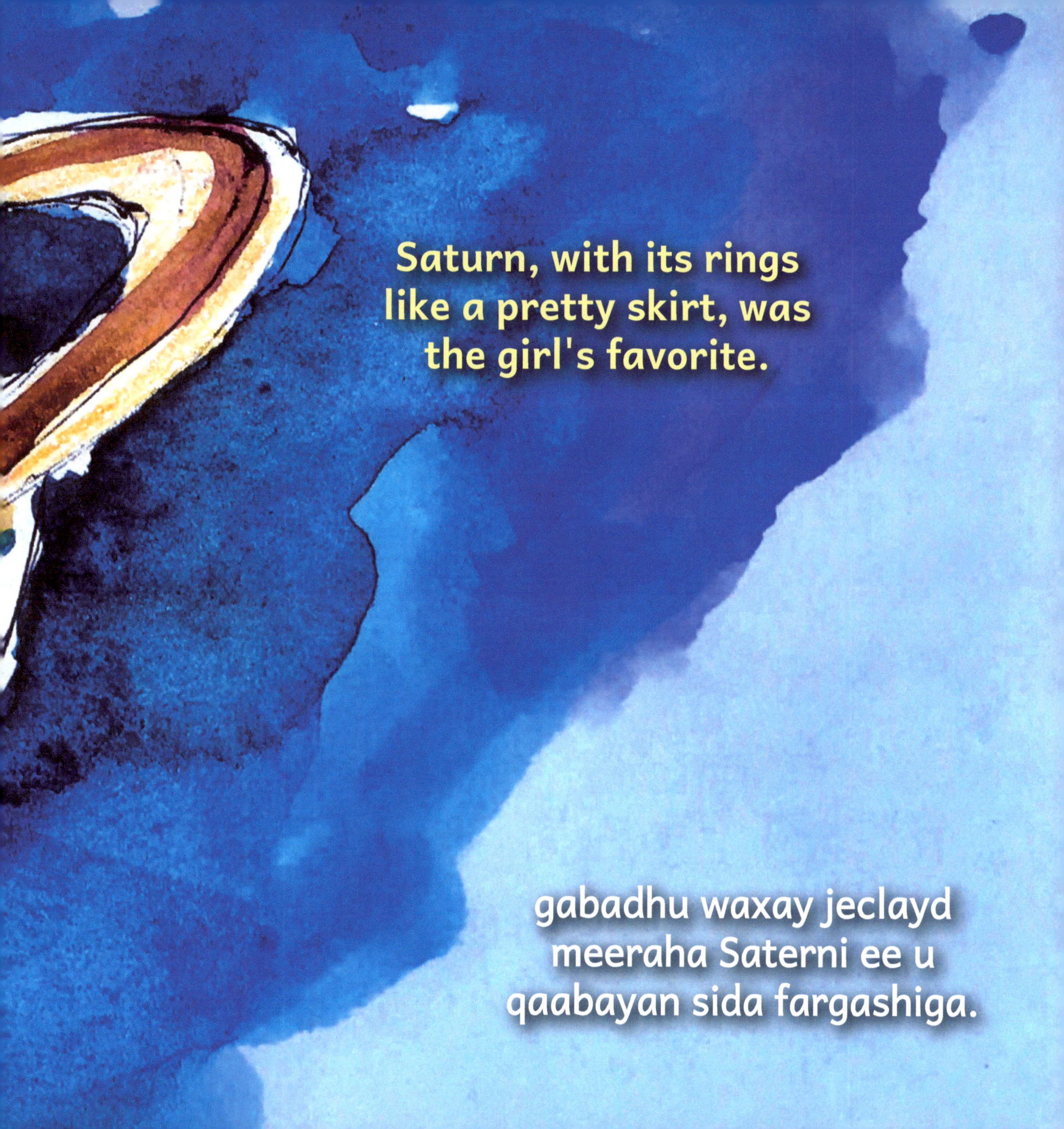

Saturn, with its rings like a pretty skirt, was the girl's favorite.

gabadhu waxay jeclayd meeraha Saterni ee u qaabayan sida fargashiga.

Her aunt liked big Jupiter with its swirling storms and all its moons.

habaryarteed waxay jeceshahay meeraha dayaxa kaas oo umuuqda dabayl kacaysa.

They were excited when they had seen all the planets.

aad ayey u farxeen markay arkeen dhamaan todobada meere.

ETHIOPIAN SPACE SCIENCE SOCIETY

"Now it's your turn to learn and dream," her aunt said. "And maybe one day you will get to go into space for Ethiopia."

gabadha yar habaryarteed ayaa kutidhi hada waa xiligaad adigu ku fikiri lahayd, waxaana suuragal ah in maalin maalmaha kamid ah aad dayaxa tagi doonto adigoo itoobiya matalaya.

"Yes," said the girl. "Until then I will keep my head in the stars, too."

"haa" ayey gabadhii yarayd habar yarteed ugu jawaabtay, laga bilaabo maanta waxaan kufikirayaa inaan dayaxa aado.

About the Story

Space is the mysterious part of our universe that many humans long to explore and know more about. When the authors were visiting Addis Ababa, they met leaders from the Ethiopian Space Science Society (ESSS), a nonprofit organization whose members are mostly students and lovers of astronomy and space science, along with a few professionals in related fields. ESSS was originally referred as "The Crazy People's Club," because many—both within and outside of Ethiopia--thought the ideas were impractical and maybe even not appropriate. But in 2012, the officials of the IAU attended an event in South Africa where the president, Mr. Robert Williams, remarked that "Ethiopia always surprises the world." The society currently has more than 10,000 members, 19 branches and 100 school space clubs.

The Ethiopian Space Program was launched in 2004 by the Ethiopian Space Science Society. In 2014 the Entoto Observatory and Research Center (EORC), established under the ESSS, built two twin 1m telescopes to be used in astronomy research and human capacity development. In 2016 the Ethiopian government created the Ethiopian Space Science and Technology Institute (ESSTI), with EORC as part of it. The vision of the ESSTI is this: "through astronomy, space science, technology, and the use of satellite data, we can contribute in the long term to the socio-economical and environmental developments of Ethiopia."

On December 20, 2019, Ethiopia launched its first microsatellite, ETRSS-1 or Ethiopian Remote Sensing Satellite, from a launching center in China. Ethiopian and Chinese officials, as well as scientists, watched a live broadcast at the Entoto Observatory and Research Center, located in the suburbs of Addis Ababa. The data from ETRSS-1 will be used by Ethiopia to see what is happening with its forest and mining resources, improve weather forecasts, and observe changes in farmland. This space program is still in its early stages, but the information will eventually help Ethiopia respond to issues and challenges.

About the Authors

Ellenore Angelidis is a public speaker, consultant, volunteer, lawyer, and aspiring writer. She stays busy with husband Michael and their three kids: two sons, Dimitri, Damian (who is an Open Hearts Big Dreams Junior Board member), and daughter, Leyla. Equalizing educational opportunities for children in Ethiopia is a passion that comes in part from being raised by two teacher parents and in part from raising an Ethiopian daughter. She founded and runs both OHBD and a new company L.E.A.D. (Lead Empower Activate Dream) LLC. Visiting Lake Tana and Bahir Dar has been a special highlight. Meeting and becoming friends with Eyayu Genet has led to amazing collaborations including three books. This is the first book where Eyayu Genet is also a co-author.

Leyla Marie Fasika Angelidis was born in bahir dar, ethiopia and joined the angelidis family in seattle as an infant. She is currently in middle school and finds it unimaginable that some kids in her birth country don't get the chance to learn to read or go to school.

She has collaborated with her family to build a library in her birth town of bahir dar and to support other literacy projects through open hearts big dreams. She is an avid reader and aspiring writer. She has co-authored a number of ohbd ready set go early reader books based on family experiences and personal interests. More recently, she is a featured spokesperson as well as helps with events and awareness building for ohbd literacy projects. Through these efforts she has learned more about her first country, language, and culture as well as positively contributed to her community in ethiopia and in the us.

She has big dreams for herself and for kids living in ethiopia (and around the world).

About the Author/Illustrator

Eyayu Genet is a visual artist and lecturer at Bahir Dar University. This book was inspired by his amazing paintings that depict life along Lake Tana and his inspiring words that are the title. He completed an MFA at Addis Ababa University and has exhibited his work in Ethiopia and various other places including Qatar, the United States, Sweden, Ecuador, and Uganda. He has been awarded the Tana media award for his contributions to promote love and peace. He's engaged with many humanitarian and social programs and working to make Bahir Dar a showcase for art in Ethiopia.

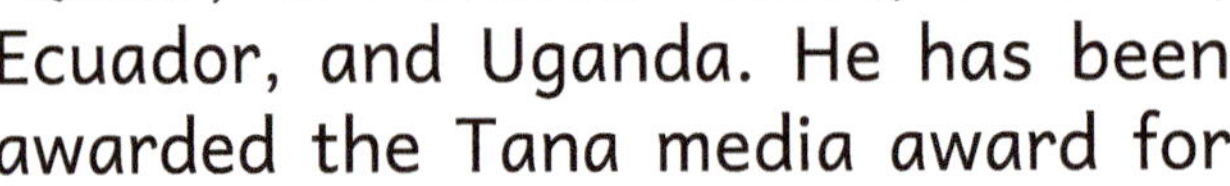

About Open Hearts Big Dreams

Open Hearts Big Dreams Fund (OHBD) was founded by Ellenore Angelidis, inspired by her Ethiopian born daughter, Leyla Marie Fasika; both are key volunteers. OHBD is a United State 501(c)(3) not-for-profit organization that believes the chance to dream big dreams should not depend on where in the world you are born. Our mission is "Inspiring and empowering youth (K-14) to reimagine their futures by providing literacy, STEAM, and leadership opportunities."

OHBD harnesses the power of collaboration. We are made up of a small number of part-time paid staff and a large number of highly motivated volunteers with advanced skills, including artistic, editorial, translation, and high-tech expertise in Ethiopia, the Diaspora and globally. Our culture of innovation means we act fast on new ideas. Since 2017, we've produced more than 700 bilingual, culturally appropriate early reader titles and a number of STEM and Model programs to increase literacy, inclusion, and leadership.

In Ethiopia, for Ethiopia; OHBD is based in the U.S. but we are committed to working with local content creators and to producing quality books in Ethiopia. Local opportunities and production builds local knowledge and capacity.

About Ready Set Go Books

Reading has the power to change lives, but many children and adults in Ethiopia cannot read. One reason is that Ethiopia doesn't have enough books in local languages to give people a chance to practice reading. Ready Set Go books wants to close that gap and open a world of ideas and possibilities for kids and their communities.

When you buy a Ready Set Go book, you provide critical funding to create and distribute more books.

Learn more at: http://openheartsbigdreams.org/book-project/

About the Language

Somali is an Afroasiatic language belonging to the Cushitic branch. Somali is spoken in Somalia, Somaliland, Djibouti, Ethiopia and Kenya. It is used as an adoptive language by a few neighboring ethnic groups and individuals. Somali was not written until the Osmanya alphabet was developed in 1920. The Latin alphabet was adopted in 1972.

About the Translation

Abdi Mohamed Hassen was born in 1987 in Sagag Distinct of Nogob Zone of the Somali Regional State. He completed primary school in Kebribayah and secondary school in Jigjiga. Abdi graduated from Addis Ababa University with BA Degree in Foreign Language and Literature(English). He also graduated MA or second degree of Educational Planning and Management at Jigjiga University. For the last 10 years has worked in the Somali Regional Education Bureau.

www.ingramcontent.com/pod-product-compliance
Lightning Source LLC
Chambersburg PA
CBHW042111110726
48006CB00002B/599

* 9 7 9 8 8 4 4 4 6 1 7 1 2 *